SCIENTIFIC HEALING AFFIRMATIONS

PARAMAHANSA YOGANANDA

GENERAL PRESS

Published by
GENERAL PRESS
4805/24, Fourth Floor, Krishna House
Ansari Road, Daryaganj, New Delhi - 110002
Ph : 011-23282971, 45795759
E-mail : generalpressindia@gmail.com

www.generalpress.in

First Edition : 2020

ISBN : 9789389716344

Published by Azeem Ahmad Khan for General Press

BESTSELLING FICTION

- 1984 by George Orwell
  Fiction/Classics, ISBN: 9789380914947
- A Tear and a Smile by Kahlil Gibran
  Fiction/Classics, ISBN: 9788180320477
- Alice's Adventures in Wonderland by Lewis Carroll
  Children's/Classics, ISBN: 9789380914046
- Animal Farm by George Orwell
  Fiction/Classics, ISBN: 9789380914701
- Black Beauty by Anna Sewell
  Children's/Classics, ISBN: 9788180320095
- Demian by Hermann Hesse
  Fiction/Classics, ISBN: 9789387669567
- Gitanjali by Rabindranath Tagore
  Fiction/Poetry, ISBN: 9789380914886
- Selected Stories of Nietzsche by Friedrich Nietsche
  Fiction/Short Stories, ISBN: 9788180320491
- Siddhartha by Hermann Hesse
  Fiction/Classics, ISBN: 9789380914145
- Tales from India by Rudyard Kipling
  Fiction/Short Stories, ISBN: 9789380914411
- The Hound of the Baskervilles by Sir Arthur Conan Doyle
  Fiction/Classics, ISBN: 9789380914534
- The Light of Asia by Sir Edwin Arnold
  Religion/Buddhism, ISBN: 9789380914923

Search the book by its ISBN

Contents

Dedicated

To My Guru Deva

Sreemat Swami Sriyukteswarji

With sincere love, reverence and devotion

Spiritual Power of Man's Word

Man's word is Spirit in man. Words are sounds occasioned by the vibrations of thoughts. Thoughts are vibrations sent forth by the Ego or Soul. Every word that leaves your mouth ought to be potent with your genuine soul vibration. Words in most people are lifeless because they are automatically put forth into the ether, without being impregnated with soul force. Too much talking, exaggeration or falsehood used in connection with words is just like shooting bullets out of a toy gun, without the gun-powder. That is why the prayers or words of such people do not produce any desired definite change in the order of things. Every word you utter you must mean it, *i.e.,* every word you put forth must represent not only Truth, but some of your realized soul force. Words without soul force are husks without the corn.

Words that are saturated with sincerity, conviction, faith and intuition are just like highly explosive vibration bombs, which when let out, are sure to explode the rocks of difficulties and create the change desired. Avoid speaking unpleasant words, even though they are true. Words must be intoned according to the convictions within. Sincere words or affirmations repeated understandingly, feelingly and willingly are sure to move the Omnipresent Cosmic Vibratory Force and render you aid in your difficulty. Only appeal to that Force with infinite confidence, casting out all doubt and the spirit of looking for the desired result. If you don't do this, your appealing attention is deflected and side-tracked from its objective mark. Besides you cannot sow the vibratory prayer seed in the soil of Cosmic Consciousness and then pick it out every minute to see if it has germinated into the desired result or not.

The God-Given Power of Man

It should be remembered that there is nothing greater in power than the Cosmic Consciousness or God. The Power of Cosmic Consciousness is greater than the power of your mind or the mind of others. Thus you should seek Its aid alone. But this does not mean that you should make yourself passive, inert or credulous, or that you should minimize the power of your mind. Remember God helps those that help themselves. He gave you will power, concentration, faith, reason and common sense to help yourself in your bodily or mental afflictions. You must use them all as you seek the Divine help. But remember in using your own will power or common sense to get rid of a difficulty or disease, you must not rely wholly on, or harness yourself solely to, your Ego and thus disconnect yourself from the Divine Force. Always during affirmations or prayer vibrations feel that you are using *your own* but *God-given* power to heal yourself or others. Always believe that it is not God only but yourself also who, as His beloved child, tries to employ His given will, reason, etc., to react on the difficult problems of life. A balance must be struck between the old idea of wholly depending on God, and the modern way of sole dependence on the ego.

During the different affirmations, the attitude of the mind should be different, e.g., will affirmations should be accompanied by strong will; feeling affirmations by devotion; reason affirmations by intelligence and devotion; imagination affirmations by firm fancy and faith. In healing others select that affirmation which is suitable to the co native, imaginative, emotional or thoughtful temperament of your patient. In all affirmations the intensity of attention comes first, but continuity and repetition count a great deal, too. Impregnate your affirmations with your devotion, will and faith, intensely and repeatedly, unmindful of the results, which will naturally come as the fruit of your labors.

During the physical curing process, the attention must not be on the disease, which always damps the faith, but on the mind. During mental cures of fear, anger, any bad habit, consciousness of failure, un-success, nervousness, etc., the concentration should be on the opposite mental quality, e.g., the cure for fear is culturing the consciousness of bravery; of anger-peace; of weakness-strength; of sickness-health.

Mental Responsibility for Chronic Diseases

In trying to get rid of a physical or mental sickness by mental or physical method one often concentrates more on the gripping power of the disease than on the possibility of cure, and thus permits the disease to be a mental as well as a physical habit. This is especially true of most cases of nervousness in which the disease is felt long after it is physically cured. Each physical activity or bodily sensation of disease or health, etc., cuts grooves on the brain-cells, which further automatically awaken certain habits of disease or health. The sub-conscious habit of disease or health consciousness exerts a strong influence on the continuity of chronic diseases. Chronic mental or physical diseases have always a deep root in the sub-conscious mind. In a mental or physical disturbance, one ought to be able to pull out its roots in the sub-conscious mind. That is why all affirmations practised by the conscious mind ought to be *impressive enough* to stay as mental habits in the subconscious mind, which would in turn again automatically influence the conscious mind. Strong conscious affirmation thus being reinforced reacts on the mind and body through the medium of the subconscious.

Still stronger conscious will or devotion affirmations not only reach the sub-conscious but the Super-conscious, the magic storehouse or factory of all miraculous mental powers.

Individual affirmations should be practised willingly, feelingly, intelligently and devotionally, once in a while loudly (when nobody is listening), but mostly mentally (not even in a whisper), with ever-increasing intensity of attention and continuity. The attention from the very beginning of affirmation must steadily increase and should never be allowed to flag. Flagging attention should be again and again brought back like a truant child and repeatedly and patiently trained to perform its given task. Attentive, intelligent repetition and patience are the creators of habits, and as such, these ought to be employed during all affirmations. Such deep and long-continued affirmations for curing chronic mental or bodily afflictions should be practised mentally until they become almost a part of one's intuitional convictions, by utterly ignoring unchanged or contrary results (if any). It is better to die (if death has to come) with the conviction of being cured than with the consciousness of a mental or bodily ailment being incurable.

Another fact should always be remembered – though death may be the necessary end of the body according to present human knowledge, still it has no fixed time, rather, even if it has, it can be modified or changed by the super-conscious power of the Soul. As such, all affirmations, it order to reach the Super-conscious, must be free from all uncertainties, doubts and inattention. Attention and Devotion are lights that can lead ever blindly uttered affirmations to the subconscious and the Super-conscious. The greater their power, the farther they can usher the vibrations of different affirmations to their subconscious or Super-conscious destinations.

What Cures? The Life Energy

Drugs, medicine, massage, spinal adjustment or electrical treatment all help to bring back the lost harmonious condition of the cells by chemicalization of the blood or stimulation of certain tissues. These are external methods that sometimes assist the life-energy to effect a cure. But they have not the power to act on a dead body, whence the life energy has vanished, for there is nothing in a dead man that can utilize the properties of medicine or electrical currents. Without the life energy, medicines, etc., cannot have any healing effect on the human body. Hence it can be seen that it is the life energy alone that can effect a cure; all external methods of stimulation can only co-operate with the life energy, and are powerless without it.

Cure According to Temperament

Imagination, convincing reason, faith, emotion or feeling, or will or conation can be employed according to the different specific imaginative or intellectual or emotional or co native nature of the individual. Few people know this. Coue wants to cure all persons by auto-suggestion only. But the diseased person of an intellectual type is not susceptible to suggestion, and can only be influenced by a metaphysical discussion of the power of consciousness over body. He needs to understand mentally the power of the mind over the body. If he can realize, for instance, that blisters can be produced by hypnosis, as Professor James points out in his "Principles of Psychology," similarly he can understand the power of the mind to cure disease. If the mind can produce ill health it can also produce good health.

Auto-suggestion is also powerless to act on the type of man characterized by strong will power.

He needs stimulation of his will power instead of his imagination if he wants to be cured of his ailment.

A case is recorded of an emotional person who had lost his power of speech, and received it back when running out of a burning house. The sudden shock produced by the sight of fire stimulated his feeling so much that he shouted out "Fire! Fire!" not remembering that hitherto he had been unable to speak. A strong emotion overcomes the power of the subconscious mental disease habit. This story illustrates the power of intense attention, which should be used in connection with affirmations for curing bodily sickness.

During my first steamer trip from India to Colombo, I was taken unawares suddenly by a spell of sea-sickness and lost the valuable contents of my stomach. I resented the experience very much because it was sprung on me without my willing permission to accept it and at a time when I was enjoying my first experience of a floating room (the cabin) and a swimming village. I determined never to be tricked again like that. I advanced my foot and planted it firmly on the floor of the cabin and commanded my will to never accept again the sea-sick experience. Later, though I was on the water for fifty days coming from Calcutta to Boston, and for a month going to Japan, and twenty-six days from Seattle to Alaska and back, I was never sea-sick again, in spite of a very rough sea which caused almost everyone else on board to be sick.

Will, or imagination, or reason, or feeling, cannot of themselves effect a physical cure.

They only act as different agents which, according to the different temperaments of different individuals, can stimulate the life energy to awaken and cure a certain ailment. In a case of paralysis of the arm, if the will or imagination is continuously stimulated, then the life energy will suddenly rush to the diseased nervous channels, curing the tissues and the paralyzed arm. The repetition of affirmations ought to be firm and continuous so that the strength of the will and imagination might be sufficient to stimulate the uncontrolled or inactive life energy.

Yogoda teaches by its art of concentration and meditation, and control of will, how to use this Life Current directly for healing one's self and others. No one should ever minimize the importance of *repeated, ever deeper* efforts of will or imagination affirmations as given in this book to effect the cure of bad habits, or mental or bodily troubles.

Two Factors in Healing

In planting a tree two things are to be considered-the proper seed, and good ground. So also in healing diseases, two factors are to be taken into account the power of the healer and the receptivity of the patient, who must respond to the healer's vibrations.

"Virtue (*i.e.,* healing power) has gone out of me," and "Thy faith has made the whole" such sayings of Jesus show that in healing both the power of the healer and the faith of the person to be healed are required.

Faith More Important than Time

Instantaneous healing of bodily, mental and spiritual diseases might occur at any moment. The accumulated darkness of ages is dispelled at once by bringing the light in, not by trying to chase the darkness out. One never can tell when he is going to be healed, so do not expect a cure at once or at some distant day. Faith, not time, will determine when the cure will be effected. Results depend on the right awakening of life energy and the mental and subconscious state of the individual. Disbelief fails to awaken the Life Energy, and this Body Doctor, Body Builder and Master Mason therefore cannot work.

Effort and attention are absolutely necessary to arouse faith or will or imagination, which, when stimulated, automatically impels the Life Energy to effect a cure. Desire or expectation for results weakens the force of attention.

Without will or faith, Life Energy remains asleep, and cure cannot take place.

It takes time to reawaken a weakened will, faith or imagination in a patient suffering from chronic disease, because his brain cells are grooved with the consciousness of disease habits... As it takes a long time to form a bad habit of disease consciousness, similarly some time is required to form a good habit of health consciousness.

Classification of Healing

1. Healing of bodily diseases.
2. Healing of such psychological diseases as fear, anger, bad habits, failure consciousness, lack of initiative and confidence, etc.
3. Healing of such spiritual diseases as ignorance, indifference, purposeless life, intellectual pride and dogmatism and theoretical metaphysics, scepticism, and contentment with the material method of existence, ignorance of the laws of life, and of his own divinity, etc.

It is of paramount importance that equal emphasis should be given to the prevention and cure of all three kinds of disease. Each causes either bodily, mental or spiritual suffering in man and must, therefore, be remedied by every suitable method of cure.

The attention of most people is fixed solely on the cure of bodily diseases, because the latter are so tangible and obvious. They do not realize that their mental troubles of fear, despair, bereavement, worry, violent anger, lack of self-control, and their spiritual suffering through ignorance of the clue to the mystery and meaning of human life are still more important and overpowering, and that all physical diseases originate in mental and spiritual in harmony. Ignorance of the laws of mental hygiene, and of the spiritual art of living are responsible for all human bodily and material suffering. If the mind is free from the mental bacteria of anger, worry, fear, etc., and the Soul is free from ignorance, no material disease or lack can follow. We do not want sickness in body, mind or soul. We do not need medicine, or mental or spiritual healing if we are well. By ignorance we break the laws of harmony by which the body was created perfectly by the Spirit, and then we seek methods of cure. We want to be disease less in every way and for that reason our whole concentration should be directed towards the prevention of physical, mental and spiritual diseases.

To Prevent Physical Disease

Obedience to God's material laws.

Do not overeat. Many dig their graves with knife and fork. Few die of starvation; most die of greediness.

Obey God's hygienic laws. The mental hygiene of keeping the mind pure is superior to physical hygiene, but the latter is very important and must not be neglected. But don't live by such mathematical laws of hygiene that the least deviation from your wonted habits upsets you.

Prevention of waste in the body by right activity and by knowledge of conservation of physical energy and of supplying the body with an inexhaustible supply of Life Current by Yogoda practices.

Charge the body cells with Life Energy by Yogoda methods.

Prevent hardening of the arteries by proper exercise.

Save the heart from overwork; fear, anger, etc., increase the heart beat. Cut down the heart beat or heart work by calmness. Give rest to the heart by the Yogoda method, and culture peace and relaxation. If we estimate the amount of blood expelled by each contraction of the ventricles of the heart at f our ounces, then the weight of the blood moved during one minute will amount to eighteen pounds. In a day it will be about 12 tons; in a year, four thousand tons. These figures indicate the enormous amount of labor expended by the heart. All other organs of the body work during the day and receive rest during the night in sleep. But the heart works even in sleep. Medical science claims that rest is received by the heart during its diastole period of expansion, amounting to about nine hours in time of the 24 hours each day. This period, however, is not rest, but is only preparation for the systole movement. The vibrations caused by the contraction of the ventricles, reverberate through the tissues of the heart during its relaxation, hence the heart cannot be said to be resting.

This effort expended daily and nightly by the heart naturally causes great wear and tear, and decay goes on until the heart is completely worn out and death ensues. Learn to sleep the big sleep (*i.e.,* conscious experience of death), wherein all the organs of involuntary motion are rested, including the heart. Control over death comes when one can consciously control and rest the motion of the heart. The rest and renewed energy given to the body by sleep is only a small indication of the wonderful calm and strength that comes through the conscious sleep, where even the heart rests.

St. Paul says in I. Corinthians, 15:31 "I protest by the rejoicing that I have in Christ, I die daily," *i.e.,* the peace that comes with Christ consciousness rests (*i.e.,* stops) the heart. Way back in these Biblical times, this great scientific truth of resting the heart and attaining immortality was known. Some years ago in India, a Yogi by the name of Sadhu Haridas was buried underground for five months under the constant supervision of European doctors, and at the end of that time he resumed breathing and returned to normal life. He had mastered the art of controlling and resting the heart.

To Prevent Mental Disease

Culture peace and faith in the Cosmic Consciousness. Free the mind from all disturbing thoughts and fill it with poise and joy. Realize the superiority of mental healing over physical healing. Abstain from acquiring bad habits, which make life miserable.

To Prevent Spiritual Disease

Knowledge of the method of spiritualizing the body by destruction of the consciousness of mortality and change. The body is materialized vibration and ought to be cognized as such. The consciousness that decay, disease or death can affect the body must be removed by scientific understanding of the underlying unifying laws of matter and spirit, and the delusive manifestation of Spirit as matter, as explained in the foregoing. Firmly believe that you are created in the image of the Father, and are therefore immortal and perfect even as He is. If a particle of matter is indestructible, as science has proved, then the soul is indestructible also. Matter undergoes change; the soul undergoes changing experiences. All changes are termed death, but the death or change of the form of a thing does not change or destroy its essence.

Apply the experiences of peace and poise received during concentration and meditation to your daily life. Maintain your equilibrium amidst trying circumstances, standing unshaken by violent emotions or adverse events. There are various methods for concentration and meditation, but Yogoda, based on Vito-Psycho-Physical methods, is the best.

Evaluation of the Science of Curative Methods

Disease is generally considered a result of external material causes-few realize that it comes through the inaction of the Life Force within. When the cell or tissue vehicle of the Life Energy is in any way affected, the Life Energy withdraws from that place and trouble consequently starts. Medicine, massage and electricity only help to stimulate the cell in such a way that the inactive Life Energy is induced to return and resume its former work of repair.

We must not be extremists in any way. We should adopt whatever methods of healing are suitable according to individual conviction. One fact should be borne in mind-medicine, food, poisons, etc., all have a definite chemical action on the blood and body. As long as one eats, why should he deny that medicines or other material aids are without effect on the body? They are useful as long as only the material consciousness is present. They have their limitations, however, because they are applied from outside. The best methods are those which help the internal Life Energy to resume its healing activities.

Medicine chemically helps the blood and tissues. Use of electrical devices is also of benefit. But neither medicine nor electricity can cure disease; they can only stimulate or coax the Life Energy back to the neglected diseased body part. Hence the introduction of a different foreign element, be it medicine or electricity or any other external aid, is undesirable if we can manage to use the Life Energy to effect a cure without employing any intermediary agent.

In massage, osteopathic treatment, adjustment of the vertebrae, Yoga postures, etc., no introduction of an outside influence is involved, and by these methods we can remove or relieve the congestion in the nerves or vertebrae and permit the free flow of Life Energy.

On the other hand, mental cure is superior to all methods of physical cure because will, imagination, faith, etc., are the different phases of consciousness which actually and directly act from within and are the motive powers that stimulate and direct the Life Energy to accomplish any definite task.

We, therefore, see that both physical methods and mental methods of cure are useful only insofar as they can influence and awaken the Life Energy. It is the Life Energy that will cure, and that method which exerts the most power over the Life Energy is the superior method. The Yogoda system teaches one to harness and direct the will to assist the actual vibrating Life Energy to any body part required. Neither physical culture methods nor mental healing can equal the marvelous results of Yogoda, which employs the will and the Life Energy directly. It is not imagination – one can feel the tingling energy throughout the body by the use of the Yogoda exercises.

Medicine may be used for little itches, sores or accidental cuts, etc. If the arm has been fractured, it is foolish to give God the trouble of joining your displaced bones when a doctor (a child of God) can fix it by a little use of his skill and knowledge of God's own laws as applied to matter. If you can instantaneously heal your broken bones by mental power it is admissable, but don't wait.

Matter does not exist in the way we usually conceive it, nevertheless, it does exist as a delusion. Dispelling delusion requires a definite method. You cannot cure a dope-fiend in a moment. Material consciousness possesses man through a law of delusion and only by following the opposite law of undoing the delusion can the material consciousness be dispelled.

The rabid medical man and the mental healer both are extremists. They are wrong because they draw a dividing line between matter and Spirit. Spirit through a series of processes of materialization became matter, hence matter proceeds from and cannot be different from its cause, the Spirit. Matter is a partial expression of Spirit-the Infinite appearing as finite, the Unlimited as limited. But since matter is nothing but Spirit in its delusive manifestation, matter cannot exist without the Spirit. Hence the Spirit exists; matter does not.

Consciousness and Vibration

Consciousness and vibratory matter are the two natures of one undivided, un-manifested Spirit. The difference between consciousness and matter is relative. The former is a deeper and the latter a grosser vibration of the one Transcendental Spirit.

The Spirit is the first cause of vibratory creation. The processes of subjective, cognitive and objectified consciousness do not exist in the Spirit. The knower, knowing and the thing known are spiritually one. By creation the hitherto un-manifested Spirit manifests two natures-one consciousness, and the other vibration. Consciousness is the vibration of Its subjective nature, and vibration is the manifestation of Its objective nature. In one phase, the Spirit appears as the universe of objectified vibratory matter, with its billions of units of Life Energy, atoms, molecules, gases, liquids, solids, etc. The other phase of the Spirit is its potential immanency in this objectified vibratory matter as Cosmic Consciousness, manifesting as individualized human consciousness with all its countless ramifications of thoughts, feelings, will, imagination, etc.

Difference Between Matter and Spirit

Hence, metaphysically speaking, the difference between matter and spirit consists in the rate of vibration, and is a difference of degree, not of kind. This point is illustrated by the fact that though all vibrations are qualitatively alike, yet vibrations from 16 to 60,000 are gross and are audible to the physical sense of hearing, whereas vibrations below 16 or over 60,000 cannot be registered by the tympanum. The vibration of consciousness is so subtle and so powerful that it cannot be detected by any gross instrument. Only consciousness can comprehend consciousness. Only conscious human beings can detect the conscious vibrations of other human beings. Those who live in a certain room impress a vibratory force on that room which may be felt by other persons.

The subtlety of the vibration of consciousness and the grossness of the vibration of matter are only superficially different. They differ in degree only, but they are so distinctly and specifically differentiated by the vibratory force of the Spirit that they appear different in kind as well as degree, to the human consciousness. Consciousness is cognized as a finer force existing within a coating of grosser vibratory force called matter; or it may be said that consciousness is the first vibration of Spirit and that matter is in turn the result of the grosser vibration of consciousness. The Ego cognizes consciousness directly and matter (*e.g.,* the body) indirectly, through consciousness (sensation, perception and conception).

There exists much misunderstanding in man's mind about the oneness that exists between matter and consciousness. The appearance of a living body and a dead body side by side in life produces in man the consciousness of the delusive difference between body and consciousness. When a man sees a dead body (*i.e.,* a body without consciousness) and a living one (*i.e.,* a body with consciousness), he begins to reason about the radical difference between body and consciousness, not remembering that the sight of a dead body or a living body may both be produced by the sustained power of a hallucination or in the dream state of the human consciousness, and so are similarly produced in life by rye power of Maya or World Illusion.

Body and Consciousness Created by Man in the Dream State

In the dream state, a sleeping man may find himself walking joyously in a beautiful garden, and perhaps he suddenly sees the dead body of a friend. He becomes stricken with grief, sheds tears, suffers from headache, feels his heart throb-or perhaps suddenly a storm blows, he is drenched in rain and becomes wet and cold. He wakes up and laughs at his illusory dream experience. What is the difference between the experiences of the sleeping man under the influence of a dream,—experiences of matter as embodied in the bodies of himself and his dead friend, the garden, heat and cold, etc., and experiences of consciousness as displayed in his recognition of himself and his friend, of his awareness of the garden, heat and cold, etc. – what, then, is the difference between these experiences of the dream state, and the experiences of his waking state? The consciousness of matter and the consciousness of consciousness are present in both cases. The sleeping man creates matter and consciousness in his dream.

World Illusion

If such a delusive creation is possible to the human consciousness, then it is not *difficult* to imagine that the infinitely powerful Cosmic Consciousness or Spirit could create by the power of Maya or World Illusion a little more permanent dream in the human consciousness, thereby making it feel the relatively permanent and paradoxical difference between matter and consciousness.

Those who seek health or happiness, or who dread disease or death or bereavement, are working under the false conviction that health is different from disease, that life is different from death, that bereavement is different from joy. Man is dreaming of these dualities, but when he awakes he finds out that these things were only a dream, a delusion of his dreaming consciousness. When man realizes his true nature, the dualities disappear and all lack is seen to be illusory, all desire vanishes.

For those who have not attained to this Cosmic Consciousness, it is useless to emphasize the importance of medical aid, or to totally ignore it; or to emphasize the importance of mental aid, or to totally ignore it. While the superiority of mental aid and the healing power of the mind over the healing power of drugs is undeniable, still the limited healing or death-dealing power of herbs and drugs can also not be denied. In employing mental aid, there is no necessity for scorn at all physical methods of cure, for they are the outcome of investigation into God's material laws.

Underlying Unity of Medical and Mental Cures

The point is, that most people either believe solely in medical or solely mental cure, and ignore the point of unity where both methods coincide. Medical laws cannot contradict mental laws, for material law is simply a projection of spiritual law. Similarly, the law that governs matter and therefore medical science is more limited and unfree than its source-therefore mental healing has a wider scope and efficacy than medicine, for the latter is a gross materialization of the former.

As long as the material consciousness of the body exists, the use of medicines and drugs cannot be dispensed with, but as soon as that material consciousness begins to diminish, the belief in drugs disappears and all bodily sufferings are seen to have their roots in the mental.

I know my master never spoke of the uselessness of drugs, yet he so trained and expanded the consciousness of his students that they placed no reliance on medicines, etc., and used only mental power to cure themselves if they fell sick. Some people, both in the East and the West, fanatically deny matter and medicine when they are so engrossed in the flesh that they feel they can't live if they miss a meal. It is inconsistent to deny the existence of matter with the same mouth that enjoys a steak for lunch every day. That state of realization in which body and mind, death and life, disease and health all appear equally delusive, is the only state wherein we can say that we don't believe in medicine, food, surgery, or the existence of matter.

Danger of Blind Denial of Matter

To teach the non-existence of matter while one is dreaming and engrossed in matter is productive of impracticality, danger and fanaticism. There is a deep-seated scientific psychological law governing the formation and breaking of the delusion of matter. Banishing delusion cannot be done by imagination and fanatic belief-it can only be accomplished by the methods of psycho-physical concentration, which gradually and consciously disengages and liberates the Soul from its identification with the material consciousness through certain definite stages of step-by-step realization.

People with material consciousness, believing in the gross body, have first to be gradually trained out of their dependence on medicine and material aids, and taught to rely more on mental aid and the immortal nature of consciousness.

Converting people with material consciousness into metaphysical fanatics gains nothing. In fact, a great deal of harm is done, for one misunderstanding leads to another, and because they fail to comprehend properly the material laws of God, which medical science has partially discovered and applied, and which these metaphysical fanatics deny in a crude, self-deceiving way, they also fail to comprehend the systematic and scientific laws of the mind, and become stubbornly fixed in their mistaken mob or congregational dogmatism. They follow an idea blindly, without satisfying the reasonable and logical side of their nature. Truth satisfies every part of man's nature, and does not include any inconsistent or inharmonious factors. Truth possessed by one man will prevail, whereas error shared by all the rest of humanity, minus that one, has to be rejected.

The Body as Materialized Vibration

The body is vibration materialized as the combination of solids, liquids and gases. Beneath the strata of flesh is the vibration of life current, present as fluid energy, and beneath it is the vibration of subtle human consciousness, which remains isolated through ignorance from the Cosmic Consciousness. In Cosmic Consciousness there is no change or death, whereas human consciousness is subject to change and limitation. The process of freeing the mind is to train it by affirmations, concentration, Yogoda, etc., so that it can gradually turn its attention away from the grosser body vibrations and its attendant changes of death, disease, etc., and feel the subtler and more stable vibration of Life Energy and consciousness on to the Cosmic Consciousness where there is no consciousness of change, *i.e.,* death, life, health, disease, etc., but where only one unchangeable consciousness of bliss reigns.

The Different States of Chanting

Remember again that the affirmations must be practised with the proper loud intonation, fading into a whisper, and above all with attention and devotion, taking the thought from the auditory sense to the understanding or conscious mind, thence to the subconscious or automatic mind, and then to the Super-conscious, with conviction about their efficacy and truth. To those who believe, these affirmations will cure them, and Yogoda will teach them how to prevent disease forever, as well as cure it.

The following chart shows the order of the various consecutive chanting states:

Conscious, Loud Chanting
Whisper Chanting
Mental Chanting

Subconscious Chanting
Super-conscious Chanting

Subconscious chanting becomes automatic, with internal consciousness only. Super-conscious chanting is when the deep internal chanting vibrations are converted into realization and are established in the super and subconscious minds as well as the conscious mind. Holding the attention unbrokenly on the real Cosmic Vibration, not on any imaginary sound, is super-conscious chanting.

Super-consciousness – Not Unconsciousness

One very important point to bear in mind is that when passing from one state of chanting to another, the attitude of the mind should likewise change, and become deeper and more concentrated. The aim is to unite chanter, chant and the process of chanting into one. The mind must sink itself into the deepest conscious state, NOT UNCONSCIOUSNESS, or absent-mindedness, or sleep, but such a focused concentrated state of absolute consciousness that all thoughts are sunk and merged into the one state, like particles drawn to an irresistible magnet.

Physiological Centers

During the different affirmations, notice should be taken of the physiological centers where the attention should be directed – *i.e.,* the heart is the center where feeling is concerned, the medulla is the source of energy, and will proceeds from the spot in the center of the forehead. Attention is unconsciously directed to those centers, *e.* g., when we feel, the attention is centered in the heart and we feel it to the exclusion of all other parts of our bodies. We want to cultivate a conscious power over the direction of attention to the centers of thought, will and feeling.

Above all, absolute unquestioning faith in God or his true devotees is the greatest method of instantaneous healing. It is better to die in the attempt to arouse that faith, than to die in good health, but with an absolute reliance on medicine or matter.

The following affirmations will greatly help congregations and individuals to understand gradually the mechanism of the human body, if they repeat them with understanding and devotion. They must dwell deeply on the inner meaning of the affirmations, and should read the discussion of Spirit and matter and mentally review it again and again.

Value of Different Methods of Cure

Prevention of disease must be the goal for which we all ought to strive. Our whole concentration ought to be on this important problem. Since many people are already suffering because they have broken spiritual, mental or physical laws of life and because many more will continue to break these laws even though they know better, it is important and necessary to consider the relative value of the different methods of curing physical diseases.

Medical science employs only physical agencies for cure, and hence has a very limited scope of action. Psycho-physical and mental cures have wider application to problems of disease, and even the most materially-minded medical man recognizes the effect of mentality on disease, and feels more confidence in his ability to cure if his patient "has faith in him."

Auto-suggestion and will-affirmations are unconscious methods of stimulating the Life Energy, but because purely mental healing methods do not consciously work with the Life Energy and use willing without establishing a physiological connection, therefore they are not efficacious in all cases of disease. If conscious will and co-operation with Life Energy be added, results are much more successful. But cure is certain if psycho-physical methods, together with will, faith and reason are blended together to direct the Life Energy and to reach the super-consciousness. Knowledge of the inherent and inseparable unity of matter and spirit solves all problems of disease.

Individual and Group Directions

Time: (For the individual) Immediately after awakening from sleep in the morning, or during the period of somnolence preceding sleep at night. (For the group) Any suitable time.

Place: Noiseless or quiet surroundings as far as possible. If the affirmations have to be used in a noisy place, just ignore the disturbance and devotedly attend to your exercise.

Method: Before starting to affirm, always free the mind of all worries and restlessness. Choose your affirmation and repeat it first loudly, then softer and more slowly, until your voice becomes a whisper. Then gradually affirm it mentally only, without moving even the tongue or the lips. Affirm mentally until you feel that you have merged into deep, unbroken concentration, not unconsciousness, but conscious continuity of uninterrupted thought.

Then if you continue with your mental affirmation, and go still deeper, you will feel a great sense of increasing joy and peace come over you. During deep concentration, your affirmation will merge into the subconscious stream, only to come back later reinforced with power to influence your conscious mind through the law of habit. During the time of experiencing ever-increasing peace, your affirmation goes deeper into the super-conscious reservoir, to return later laden with unlimited power not only to influence your conscious mind but also to materially fulfil your desires. Doubt not and you shall witness the miracle of this scientific faith.

During group affirmations for curing physical or mental disease in self or others, care should be taken to affirm with an even tone, even men force, even concentration and even sense of faith and peace. Weaker minds lessen the united force born of such affirmations and can even side-track this flood of force from its super-conscious destination. By all means do not make any bodily movements or become mentally restless or disturb your neighbor. Merely keeping still is not enough, you must remember your concentration or restlessness will materially affect the desired result favorably or unfavorably.

The following affirmation-seeds are impregnated with the Soul's inspiration, and they should be watered by your faith and concentration and sown in the soil of super-conscious peace, in order to set up inner motile vibrations that will help their desired germination.

There are many processes involved between the sowing of the affirmation-seed and its fruition. All the conditions of its growth must be fulfilled in order to produce the desired result. The affirmation-seed must be a living one, free from the cankers of doubt, restlessness or inattention; it should be sown in the minds and hearts of people, with faith, concentration, devotion and peace; it should be watered with deep, fresh repetitions.

Always avoid mechanical repetition. This meaning is found in the Biblical commandment, "Take not the name of the Lord thy God in vain." Repeat affirmations firmly and with intensity and sincerity, until such power is gained that one command, one strong urge from yourself would be sufficient to change your body cells or move your Soul to the performance of miracles.

Preliminary Rules to be Observed before Affirmations

1. Sit facing North or East.
2. Close your eyes (concentrating your attention on the medulla, unless otherwise directed). Keep spine erect, chest high, abdomen in. Relax completely. Take deep breaths and exhale thrice.
3. Relax the body and keep it motionless. Empty the mind of all restless thoughts, and withdraw it from all sensations of bodily weight, temperature and sounds, etc.
4. Fill your mind with devotion and with will, feeling the former in the heart and the latter in its physiological center of generation in between the eyebrows. Cast away anxiety, distrust, worry. Realize calmly

that the Divine Law works and is All-Powerful only when you do not shut it out by doubt or disbelief. Faith and concentration allow it to operate unhampered. Hold the thought that all bodily states are changeable and curable and that the consciousness of anything being chronic is a delusion.

5. Forget what it is that you want to be healed.
6. In group affirmations the leader should read the affirmations rhythmically while standing. The audience should repeat after him with his same rhythm and intonation.

General Healing Affirmation

On every altar of feeling
Thought and will
Thou art sitting
Thou art sitting.
Thou art all feeling, will and thought.
Thou dost guide them,
Let them follow, let them follow
Let them be as Thou art.
In the temple of consciousness
There was the Light-Thy Light
I saw it not, now I see
The temple is light, the temple is whole.
I slept and dreamt the temple broke
With fear, worry, ignorance;

I slept and dreamt the temple broke
With fear, worry, ignorance.
Thou hast waked me
Thou hast waked me
Thy Temple is whole
Thy Temple is whole.
I want to worship
Thee I want to worship
Thee in the heart
In the star
In the body cell I love Thee
In the electron I play with Thee.
I wish to worship Thee
In body, star, star-dust nebulae
Thou art everywhere, everywhere
I worship Thee.
Celestial will of thine
As human will of mine
Doth shine, doth shine
In me, in me, in me, in me.
I shall not say 'tis Thy Will
That I am wrong or I am ill
'Tis my will divorced from Thee
That makes me bound, unfree.
I will wish, I will will
I will work, I will drill

Not led by Ego but by Thee
But by Thee, but by Thee
I will work, exert my will
But charge my will
With Thy own Will, with Thy own Will
Make us little children, O Father
Even as Thy Kingdom contains such.
Thy love in us is perfection
Even as Thou art whole, so are we holy.
In body and mind we are healthy
Even as Thou art, even as Thou art.
Thou art perfect
We are Thy children.
Thou art everywhere
Where'er Thou art, perfection's there
Thou art sitting in every altar cell
Thou art in all my body cells
They are whole, they are perfect
They are whole, they are perfect.
Make me feel Thou art there
In them all, in them all,
Make me feel, they are perfect
Each and all, each and all.
Life of my life, Thou art whole
Thou art everywhere,
In my heart, in my brain

In my eyes, in my face
In my limbs and all.
Thou dost move my feet,
They are whole, they are whole.
My calves and thighs
They are whole, for Thou art there
My thighs are held by Thee
Lest I fall, lest I fall.
They are whole, for Thou art there
They are whole, for Thou art there.
Thou art in my throat
Mucous membrane, abdomen
Glistens with Thee
These are whole, for Thou art there.
In my spine, Thou dost sparkle
It is whole, it is whole.
In my nerves Thou dost flow
They are whole, they are whole.
In my veins and arteries
Thou dost float, Thou dost float,
They are whole, they are whole.
Thou art fire in my stomach
Thou art fire in my intestines
They are whole, they are whole.
Even as Thou art my own
So am I Thy own.

Thou art perfect
Thou art I, Thou art I.
Thou art my brain –
It is shining, it is whole,
It is whole, it is whole, it is whole.
Let my fancy flow free
Let my fancy flow free.
I am ill when so I think
I am well when so I think,
Every hour, O every day
In body, mind, in every way
I am whole, I am gay
I am whole, I am gay.
I dreamt a dream that I was ill
I woke and laughed to find me still Bedewed with tears
Of joy, not sadness,
To find I dreamt of sickness.
For I am whole, I am whole.
Let me feel
Thy loving thrill, Thy loving thrill. Thou art my Father
I am Thy Child
Good or naughty
I am Thy child.
Let the feel Thy healthy thrill
Let me feel Thy wisdom's will.
Let me feel Thy wisdom's will.

Thought-Affirmation

Concentrate Thought on the forehead, and repeat the following:

I think my life to flow
I know my life to flow
From brain to all my body to flow.
Streaks of light do shoot
Through my tissue-root.
The flood of Life through vertebrae
Doth rush through spine in froth and spray
The little cells all are drinking
Their tiny mouths all are shining
The little cells all are drinking
Their tiny mouths all are shining.

Will-Affirmation

Concentrate will[1] on the Medulla and on the spot between the eyebrows, simultaneously, and repeat the following, first loudly and then gradually in whispers:

I will my life to charge
With Godly will I will it charge
Through my nerves and muscles all
My tissues, limbs and all,
With vibrant tingling fire
With burning joyous power
In blood and glands
By sovran command
I bid you flow
By my command

---

1. The conscious will direction of the Life Energy is only possible by the technique taught in the Yogoda lessons.

I bid you glow
By my command
I bid you glow.

For the Development and Right Guidance of Reason and Cure of Dull Intelligence

1. Read, mark and inwardly digest.
2. Reason about good things.
3. Adopt the best plan you can offer to yourself by the exercise of reason.
4. If you read one hour, then write for two hours, and think for three hours. This proportion should be observed in the effort to culture reason.
5. Obey the mental laws that are given to you by God for developing your reason.

6. If these affirmations are uttered with soul force behind them they will develop the innate intelligence which the modern psychologists claim is limited and incapable of expansion.

By obeying material laws and believing them to be controlled by a superior spiritual law, one can rise above them and be wholly guided by them. This transcendental superiority of spiritual laws over material laws cannot be realized by anyone who thinks he can overcome material laws by crudely denying their existence and acting against them.

Concentrate beneath the skull, feeling weight of the brain within it:

In wisdom's chambers
Thou dost roam
Thou art the reason in me
Thou dost roam and wake
Each lazy little cell of brain
To receive, to receive

The good that mind and senses give
The knowledge that Thou dost give.
Myself will think, myself will reason I won't trouble
Thee for thought
But lead Thou when reason errs
To its goal lead it right.

Wisdom-Affirmation

Oh Father Divine,
Oh Mother Divine
Oh Master mine,
Oh Friend Divine
I came alone, I go alone

With Thee alone, with Thee alone
With Thee alone, with Thee alone.

O Thou didst make a home for me
Of living cells; a home for me.

This home of mine is home of thine
Thy life did make this home
Thy strength did make this home.

Thy home is perfect, Thy home is perfect.

I am Thy child, Thou art my Father
We both do dwell, we both do dwell
In the temple same
In this temple of cells
O in this temple of cells.
Thou art always here
O on my throbbing altar near.

I went away, I went away

With darkness to play, with error to play,
A truant child, I went away.
Home I came with Darkness dark Home
I came with matter's muddy mark.
Thou art near, I cannot see
Thy home is perfect, I cannot see.
I am blind, Thy Light is there
'Tis my fault that I cannot see
O 'tis my fault that I cannot see.
Beneath the darkness line

Thy Light doth shine Thy Light doth shine.

Together, Thy Light and Darkness cannot stay, cannot stay.
Together, wisdom, ignorance

Cannot stay, cannot stay.
Conjure away, O lure away

The darkness away
My darkness away.

My body cells are made of light
My fleshly cells are made of Thee

They are perfect, for thou art perfect they are healthy, for thou art health they are spirit, for thou art so they are immortal, for thou art living.

Success Affirmations

(For Healing of Unsuccess Consciousness)

Success comes by obeying the Divine and material laws. Material and spiritual success both must be attained. Material success consists in acquiring all the necessities of life. Ambition for money making should be utilized to improve society, country and the world. Make all the money you can by improving your community or country or the world, but never do so by acting against their interests.

Remember there are mental, sub-conscious and super-conscious laws for success, and for fighting failure.

The subconscious method of success is to repeat the affirmations intensely and attentively immediately before and after sleep.

If you want Divine Law or super-conscious power to help you, do not stop your conscious efforts, nor should you *rely* wholly on your own natural abilities. Use effort consciously by trying and planning to succeed and by fighting failure, feeling at the same time that the Divine Law is helping your efforts to successfully reach their destination. This method establishes a conscious connection with the Divine. Think that as you are the child of God you have access to all things that belong to your Father. Doubt not; when you want anything, cast away the consciousness of failure, realize that all things are your own. Subconscious habits of ignorance and disbelief in this law have deprived us of our Divine heritage. Those who crave to utilize the resources of Divine Supply must destroy this wrong mentality by steady effort saturated with infinite confidence.

Thus when the conscious, subconscious and super-conscious methods of success are combined, success will surely come. Try again, no matter how many times you have tried for it unsuccessfully.

Material Success Affirmation

Thou art my Father
Success and joy
I am Thy child
Success and joy

All the wealth of this earth
All the riches of the universe

Belong to Thee, belong to Thee.
I am Thy child

The wealth of earth and universe
Belongs to me, belongs to me
O belongs to me, belongs to me.
I lived in thoughts of poverty

And wrongly fancied I was poor
So I was poor.

Now I am home and thy consciousness has made me wealthy, made me rich. I am success, I am rich thou art my treasure, I am rich, I am rich.

Thou art everything,
Thou art everything
Thou art mine

I have everything, I have everything
I am wealthy, I am rich
I have everything,
I have everything
I possess all and everything
Even as Thou dost, even as Thou dost
I possess everything,
I possess everything.
Thou art my wealth
I have everything.

Spiritual success consists in contacting Cosmic Consciousness consciously, and in maintaining your peace and poise no matter what irremediable events of life, like death of friends or other bereavement, come to you. In case of the separation of one of your dear ones by the law of Nature, you should not sorrow, but should rather thank God that He gave you the great privilege of tending and befriending and keeping in your charge one of His dear ones. Spiritual success comes by understanding the mystery of all the events of life, and by looking upon all things cheerfully and courageously, with the realization that everything is marching towards the highest goal. Ignorance should be healed by knowledge.

Spiritual Success Affirmation

(For Healing the Soul's Ignorance)

Thou art knowledge
And Thou dost know
The cause and end of all things.
I am Thy child

I want to know Life's true mystery
Life's true joyous duty

Thy knowledge in me shall show
All things that
Thou dost know that
Thou dost know.

In healing, as we have previously said, imagination, will, faith, reason and feeling all stimulate the disturbed Life Energy, which can actually internally electrify the diseased body cells and restore them to their original healthy condition. Hence those that want to scientifically heal ought to know the laws of visualizing and controlling this Life Energy. In healing others, one has to have control over his Life Energy and project a current into his patient's body which stimulates and harmonizes the disturbed Life Energy of the patient by the power of will or imagination. Healing cannot be done by chance – the great healers can watch the actual psycho-physical laws of nature operating in the body of patient during the process of curing.

Affirmation for the Eyes

Concentrate with closed eyes first on the medulla, then feel the power of vision in the eyes flowing through the optical nerves into the retina. Concentrate on the retina. Dilate eyes and relax.

Psychological Success Affirmations

I am brave,
I am strong.
Perfume of success thought
Blows in me, blows in me.
I am cool,
I am calm I am sweet,
I am kind I am love,
I am sympathy
I am charming and magnetic
I am pleased with all
I wipe the tears and fears of all
I have no enemy

Though some think they are so.

I am the friend of all.
I have no habits,
In eating, dressing, behaving
I am free, I am free.

I command Thee, O Attention

To come and practise concentration
On things I do, on works I do.
I can do everything

When so I think, when so I think.
In church or temple, prayer mood

My vagrant thoughts against me stood
And held my mind from reaching thee
And held my mind from reaching thee
Teach me to own again,
O own again
My matter-sold mind and brain
That I may give them to thee
In prayer and ecstasy
In meditation and reverie.
I shall worship thee in meditation

In the mountain breast and seclusion.
I shall feel thy energy
Flowing thru my hands in activity
Lest I lose thee

I shall find thee in activity.

In the peaceful lake of peace

In the hour of wisdom's dawn.
The light of thine
O shines through mine
Through past, present and future time I command you

My eyes two
Be one and single
Be one and single

To see all and know all
To make my body shine
To make my mind shine
To make my soul shine.

Turn the eyeballs upward, then downward, then to the left, then to the right. Then rotate them from left to right, and right to left. Fix the attention of the eyes on the spot in the middle of the forehead, thinking that the Life Energy flows into and transforms both eyes into two searchlights. This exercise is also beneficial physically for the eyes.

I bid you
O rays of blue

To glide through my optic nerves
And show me true, and show me true

'His Light is there
His Light is there.
Through my eyes
Thou dost peep
Thou dost peep.

They are whole, they are perfect.

One above and two below

Eyes three, eyes three

Through you unseen, what light doth flee
Through you unseen, what light doth flee.
Lotus eyes, weep no more weep no more

The storms thy petals hurt no more.
Come quick and glide like swans
In the blithesome water of Bliss

"Spiritual eye.

For Regulating Sex Force

Before retiring at night, wipe hands, feet, armpits, navel, face, medulla and all body openings with a wet towel. Do this regularly.

During bodily excitement, draw a deep breath and exhale deeply. Repeat 6 to 15 times and then quickly go amidst crowds of people or your superiors.

Through pollen and stamen
Thou dost create the flowers pure
Through my parents pure my body
Thou didst bring Even as
Thou art the creator
Of all good things so are we.

Teach us to create

In sacredness, in holiness Noble ideas or noble souls in holiness

As need be, as need be. Thou art sexless

We are sexless, we are sexless.
Thou didst create us in purity.
Teach us to create in sacredness
Noble thoughts or children
Wrought in thy image.

The body is like a garden overflowing with charming fruits of the senses, of sound, sight, taste, smell and touch. The divinity in man warns him against over-indulgence and immoderation in the use of any of these sense-fruits, but especially against the wrong use of the apple of sex-force, situated in the center of this bodily Garden of Eden. By allowing the serpent of evil curiosity and the Eve or weak feminine nature in him to tempt him to transgress the law of regulated and non-identified sense experience, man is driven from his perfect garden of Bliss Consciousness and loses the joy of self-control. The unnatural awakening of sex consciousness brings in the fig leaf or sin consciousness of shame. Parents desiring children should be particularly careful of confining their attention to the creative end and to ignore the means to that end. The charm of sex communion should not be used by man for its own sake.

For Curing Bad Habits

1. Good habits are your best helpers; preserve their force by stimulating them with good actions.
2. Bad habits are your worst enemies; against your will they make you do things which hurt you most. They are detrimental to your physical, social, mental, moral and spiritual happiness. Starve bad habits by refusing to give them any further food of bad actions.
3. True freedom consists in doing things, *i.e.,* eating, reading, helping, etc., in accordance to right judgment and choice of will; not in being compelled by habits.

   Eat what you should eat and not necessarily what you are used to. Do what you ought, not what your habits dictate.

4. Good and bad habits both take some time to acquire force. Powerful bad habits can be displaced by opposite good habits if the latter are, patiently cultured.
5. First crowd out all bad habits by good habits in everything, then culture the consciousness of being free from all habits in eating, working, etc.

Thou art in law
Thou art above all laws

I am thy child,
I love thy law
Above all laws am I
Even as thou art
Above all laws am I

Oh yes brave good soldier habits
Drive away the dark, dark habits
Drive away the dark, dark habits.
I am free, I am free
I have no habits, I have no habits

I will do what is right, I'll do what's right
Un-commanded by habits' might
I am free, I am free

I have no habits, I have no habits.

Physical Exercise for Stomach

Bend down while holding the arms of a chair. Exhale breath completely and cave in the stomach and abdomen as far as possible (as near the backbone as possible). Then throw them out (bulging them) while inhaling. Repeat 12 times. This exercise helps the peristaltic action of the stomach and removes its ailments.

While the superiority of mental over physical cure is undeniable, nevertheless these few physical exercises are included in this book for the benefit of those who desire to combine both methods.

Exercise for the Teeth

With eyes closed clinch the upper and lower left teeth together, then the upper and lower right teeth together, then the front upper and lower teeth together. Then clinch the entire set of upper and lower teeth. Hold each state for one or two minutes, concentrating on the "clinching teeth sensation" thinking the healing energy is vitalizing all the roots of the teeth and is removing all inharmonious conditions.

INTERNATIONAL BESTSELLER

SIDDHARTHA

by Hermann Hesse

Price	:	Rs. 225
Pages	:	168
Size	:	8x5.25 inches
Binding	:	Paperback
Language	:	English
Subject	:	Fiction/Classics
ISBN	:	9789380914145

Siddhartha is an allegorical novel by Hermann Hesse which deals with the spiritual journey of an Indian boy called Siddhartha during the time of the Buddha. The book was written in German, in a simple, yet powerful and lyrical style. It was first published in 1922, after Hesse had spent some time in India in the 1910s.

The story revolves around a young man who leaves his home and family on a quest for the Truth. Embarking on a journey that takes him from the austerities of renunciation to the profligacy of wealth. That leads him through the range of human experiences from hunger and want, to passion, pleasure, pain, greed, yearning, boredom, love, despair and hope. A journey that leads finally to the river, where he gains peace and eventually wisdom. This is the story of Siddhartha as told by Nobel Laureate Hermann Hesse in his most influential work.

Hermann Hesse:

Hermann Hesse (b. 1877) was a German-born Swiss poet and author, best known for writing the novels *Steppenwolf*, *Siddhartha*, and *The Glass Bead Game*. He was awarded the Nobel Prize for Literature in 1946. His themes focus on man's struggle to break away from the rigid structures of civilization and follow his essential and inner spirit. For this, Hesse became a literary cult figure.

INTERNATIONAL BESTSELLER

THE BHAGAVAD GITA

Translated by

SIR EDWIN ARNOLD

Price	:	Rs. 195
Pages	:	128
Size	:	8x5.25 inches
Binding	:	Paperback
Language	:	English
Subject	:	Religion & Sprituality
ISBN	:	9789380914275

The Bhagavad Gita, meaning the Song of the Lord, is in the form of a poetic dialogue between Arjuna and Krishna. It is part of the great Indian epic 'The Mahabharata', and is one of the major religious documents of the world. It reveals how human beings accumulate 'Karma' as a result of their actions in innumerable incarnations, and how to achieve liberation through devotion and knowledge.

The dialogue, which takes place on the eve of an historic battle, probes the nature of God and what man should do to reach him. As *The Bhagavad Gita* unfolds, this majestic poem provides a fascinating synopsis of the religious thought and experience of India through the ages. This book offers the classic English verse translation by Sir Edwin Arnold (1832-1904), long admired for its evocation of the true feeling of the original poetry.

Sir Edwin Arnold:

Sir Edwin Arnold (1832-1904), was an English author. After serving as principal of the government college in Pune, India, he joined (1861) the staff of *The London Daily Telegraph.* He won fame for his blank-verse epic *The Light of Asia* (1879), dealing with the life of Buddha. The poem was attacked for its alleged distortion of Buddhist doctrine and for its tolerant attitude toward a non-Christian religion. Besides other volumes of poetry, he wrote a number of picturesque travel books and translated Asian literature, inclding *The Bhagavad Gita.*

OTHER BOOKS YOU MAY LIKE

- A Christmas Carol by Charles Dickens, ISBN: 9788193545874
- Anthem by Ayn Rand, ISBN: 9789389157079
- Apni Chhamta Pehchaniye by NK Sondhi, ISBN: 9788193545843
- As a Man Thinketh by James Allen, ISBN: 9788180320262
- Awakened Imagination by Neville Goddard, ISBN: 9789389157086
- Be What You Wish by Neville Goddard, ISBN: 9789387669550
- Becoming a Writer by Dorothea Brande, ISBN: 9789389157093
- Believe in Yourself by Joseph Murphy, ISBN: 9789388118385
- Civilization and Its Discontents by Sigmund Freud, ISBN: 9789387669499
- Feeling is the Secret by Neville Goddard, ISBN: 9789389157109
- Gita According to Gandhi by Mahatma Gandhi, ISBN: 9788180320040
- Gravity by George Gamow, ISBN: 9789388118484
- Great Speeches of Abraham Lincoln by Abraham Lincoln, ISBN: 9789380914336
- How to Attract Money by Joseph Murphy, ISBN: 9789388118408
- How to be filled with the Holy Spirit by A. W. Tozer, ISBN: 9789389157116
- How to Dev Self Conf and Imp Pub Speaking by Carnegie, ISBN: 9789387669000
- How to Enjoy Your Life and Your Job by Dale Carnegie, ISBN: 9789387669017
- How to Stop Worrying and Start Living by Dale Carnegie, ISBN: 9789380914817
- Julius Caesar by William Shakespeare, ISBN: 9789380914374
- Macbeth by William Shakespeare, ISBN: 9789380914343
- Madhubala by Manju Gupta, ISBN: 9789380914961
- Meditations by Marcus Aurelius, ISBN: 9789388118736
- Mein Kampf (My Struggle) by Adolf Hitler, ISBN: 9789380914855
- Metamorphosis by Franz Kafka, ISBN: 9788180320057
- Mother by Maxim Gorky, ISBN: 9788180320330
- My Experiments with Truth by Mahatma Gandhi, ISBN: 9789387669291

Develop your reading habit | **Gift books to your friends**

OTHER BOOKS YOU MAY LIKE

OTHER BOOKS YOU MAY LIKE

- The Little Prince by Antoine De Saint-Exupéry, ISBN: 9788180320590
- The Magic of Believing by Claudie Bristol, ISBN: 9789388118149
- The Magic of Faith by Joseph Murphy, ISBN: 9789388118743
- The Miracles of Your Mind by Joseph Murphy, ISBN: 9788180320743
- The Origin of Species by Charles Darwin, ISBN: 9788180320453
- The Path of Prosperity by James Allen, ISBN: 9789387669512
- The Power of Awareness by Neville Goddard, ISBN: 9789387669406
- The Power of Concentration by Theron Q. Dumont, ISBN: 9789388118064
- The Prince by Niccolò Machiavelli, ISBN: 9789387669024
- The Prophet by Kahlil Gibran, ISBN: 9789380914022
- The Psychopathology of Everyday Life by Sigmund Freud, ISBN: 9789388118071
- The Pursuit of God by A. W. Tozer, ISBN: 9789389157147
- The Quick and Easy Way to Effe. Speaking by D. Carnegie, ISBN: 9789387669031
- The Seven Laws of Teaching by John Milton Gregory, ISBN: 9789387669413
- The Story of My Life by Helen Keller, ISBN: 9789380914541
- The Upanishads by Swami Paramananda, ISBN: 9789388118750
- The Wit and Wisdom of Gandhi by Mahatma Gandhi, ISBN: 9789380914039
- Think and Grow Rich by Napoleon Hill, ISBN: 9788180320255
- Thought Vibration by William Walker Atkinson, ISBN: 9789389157154
- Three Men in a Boat by Jerome K. Jerome, ISBN: 9789380914442
- Treasure Island by Robert Louis Stevenson, ISBN: 9788193545881
- Up From Slavery by Booker T. Washington, ISBN: 9789380914565
- Wake Up and Live! by Dorothea Brande, ISBN: 9789387669574
- Walden and Civil Disobedience by Henry David Thoreau, ISBN: 9788180320507
- Wuthering Heights by Emily Brontë, ISBN: 9788193545898
- Your Faith is Your Fortune by Neville Goddard, ISBN: 9789389157161

Develop your reading habit | **Gift books to your friends**